1776

UNITED STATES
International Exhibition.
PHILADELPHIA

May 10th.   Nov. 10th.

PACKAGE TICKET.

No.

ADMIT THE BEARER.

22330

David G. Yates

GENL. MANAGER DEPT. OF ADMISSIONS.

CENTENNIAL PHILADELPHIA

by Richard R. Nicolai

Bryn Mawr Press, Inc.
Bryn Mawr, Pennsylvania

ACKNOWLEDGEMENTS

I owe a debt of gratitude to the Fairmount Park Commission and to Robert C. McConnell, director of the Commission, for encouragement in writing this book and for affording me the opportunity to work in a Centennial atmosphere in Memorial Hall. And I wish to thank my family for their sympathetic understanding during the many hours spent in researching and preparing this book. It is to them that *Centennial Philadelphia* is dedicated.

The Glorious Enterprise, written by John Maass, an information officer for the City of Philadelphia, is a superb account of the Centennial and is recommended to anyone desiring a more detailed account of America's 100th birthday party.

Richard R. Nicolai

IF YOU VISIT...

If you visit Fairmount Park, you should stop at the only two buildings still remaining from the Centennial. Ohio House, at Belmont Avenue and States Drive, has been converted into a visitors' information center for Fairmount Park.

In the basement of Memorial Hall is a magnificent scale model of the entire Centennial Exhibition. The model measures 19 feet by 31 feet and depicts in excellent detail all 249 of the buildings which were on the Centennial grounds during 1876. It was built by the staff of Spring Garden Institute shortly after the Centennial, and its $25,000 cost was paid for by John Baird, a member of the Centennial Board of Finance. It was presented to the City of Philadelphia in 1890.

International Standard Book Number: 0-89299-001-5
Library of Congress Catalog Card Number: 76-1560

Bryn Mawr Press, Inc.
Box 690
Bryn Mawr, Pa. 19010

❧ CONTENTS ❧

Souvenir sellers were entrancing little children even a hundred years ago.

1

THE PARTY OF THE CENTURY

Uniformed boys sold guide books throughout the Centennial grounds (above). Workmen are completing the statues of Pegasus in front of Memorial Hall (left).

"One hundred years ago our country was new and but partially settled."

With that simple sentence, scarcely audible above the roar of the 100,000 gathered revelers, President Ulysses S. Grant began his brief opening remarks and the Centennial of 1876 was under way.

Though a hundred years had indeed passed since the nation's beginning, the United States was still rather sparsely settled as President Grant spoke on May 10, 1876. The American flags that fluttered everywhere throughout the Centennial grounds in Philadelphia's Fairmount Park bore only 37 stars, and the combined population of all the states and territories was only slightly more than 40 million.

Ten million visitors came to Philadelphia from around the world to celebrate the 100th birthday of what was rapidly becoming one of the greatest nations of all time.

But ironically, while top-hatted gentlemen and their ladies were strolling through the Centennial grounds, two thousand miles away in Montana the Sioux Indians were also celebrating. By annihilating General George A. Custer and his troops, the Sioux had just inflicted the worst defeat in the history of the U. S. Cavalry. Word of the massacre reached horrified Philadelphians on July 6, two days after the mammoth Fourth of July celebration.

The Centennial year also marked a victory for

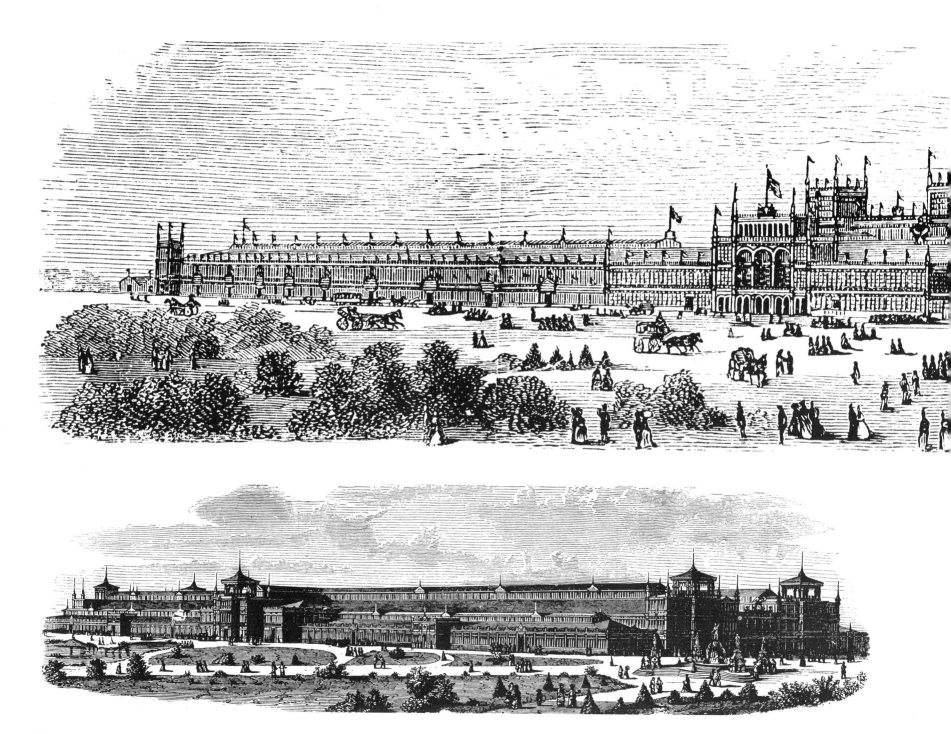

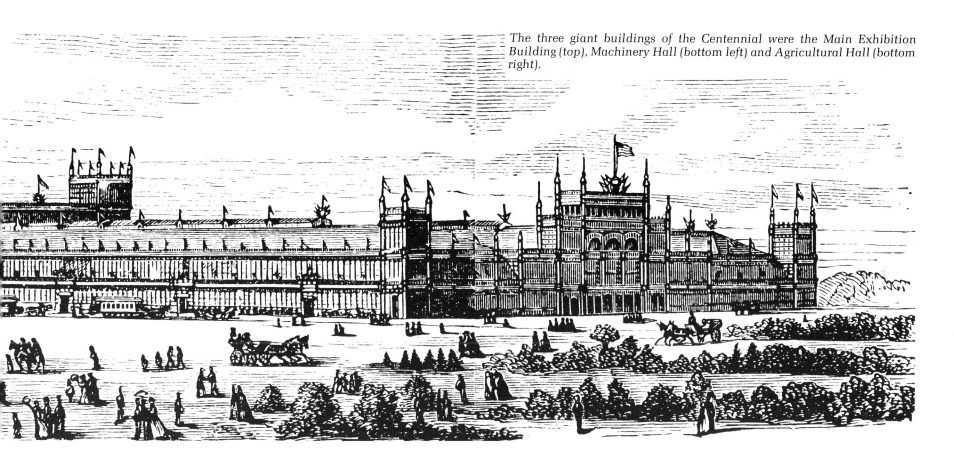

The three giant buildings of the Centennial were the Main Exhibition Building (top), Machinery Hall (bottom left) and Agricultural Hall (bottom right).

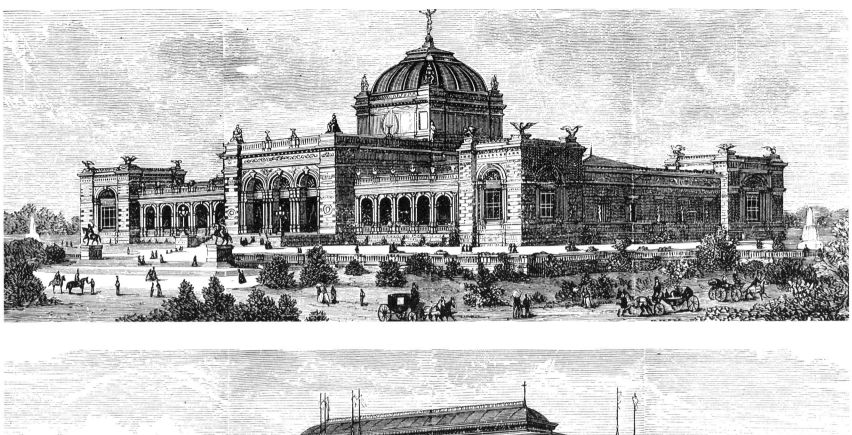

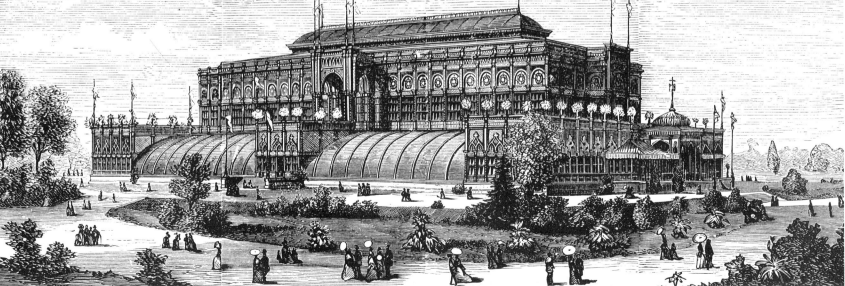

10

The two buildings designed to be permanent were Memorial Hall (top left) and Horticultural Hall (bottom left and below), with its elaborate Moorish architecture.

The immense Main Exhibition Building has been completed, and exhibitors are busy moving in their displays. This building was the largest structure in the world at the time. It featured thousands of international, state, commercial and industrial exhibits.

another "minority." It was the scene—however quietly—of the first successful women's liberation fight, appropriately led by the great-granddaughter of Benjamin Franklin.

The fair was the first time the head of a foreign state—Dom Pedro of Brazil—had ever visited America. And it marked the introduction of Alexander Graham Bell's telephone.

Indeed, the Centennial of 1876 was a Coming of Age for America. Following closely on the heels of a Civil War which had almost torn apart the nation, the giant celebration was a successful attempt to tell the rest of the world that America was stronger than ever, and that it had every intention of becoming even stronger.

Never before and never since was there such a birthday party for an entire nation as the one staged in 1876 in Philadelphia's placid Fairmount Park.

*   *   *

"Whilst proud of what we have done, we regret that we have not done more. Our achievements have been great enough, however, to make it easy for our people to acknowledge superior merit wherever found," concluded President Grant in his low-key opening statement.

Born of revolution, tested by a bitter Civil War and the recent assassination of its wartime President, the United States needed a celebration. And celebrate it did. The Civil War was a fading decade removed and a new spirit of nationalism abounded across the nation—and Philadelphia was to be the focus of it all in 1876.

After attempts by some Congressmen to discredit Philadelphia as a fit and progressive enough city to host the Centennial, Philadelphia easily won out over New York and Boston as host for the celebration.

Selected as the fairgrounds site was the city's beautiful Fairmount Park. "Your Central Park is a cabbage-garden by comparison," author Lafcadio Hearn later wrote to a New York friend in praise of Fairmount Park. Some 450 acres of the park were set aside for the Centennial, on loan from the Fairmount Park Commission, and 236 acres were eventually enclosed for the fairgrounds. Fifteen foreign nations and 24 states, including the former "Rebel" states of

13

Agricultural Hall (above) looked like several giant barns tied together. The interior view of Machinery Hall (left) shows how railroad sidings were extensively used during construction of the Centennial buildings.

Arkansas and Mississippi, constructed buildings on the fairgrounds.

The Centennial marked the beginning of the separate "pavilion" concept for world's fairs that still exists today. Previous world's fairs in London (1851 and 1862), Paris (1855 and 1867) and Vienna (1873) featured a single large exhibition hall.

The Centennial had its large buildings, too, in combination with the smaller pavilions. State and foreign nations that didn't build their own structures on the fairgrounds exhibited within the large exhibition halls and specialty buildings.

The Main Exhibition Hall was the largest of the five big exhibition buildings on the fairgrounds. And it was the largest building anywhere in the world at the time, covering more than 21 acres. Designed to measure 1876 feet in length to commemorate the year, it was said to be a few feet shorter or longer by those who took the time to measure.

And measure they did, apparently to see how they measured up to their European forerunners. America was determined that its fair would be bigger and better than its European predecessors.

The Main Exhibition Hall was a gigantic structure containing four miles of pipe, eight and a half million pounds of iron and seven million feet of lumber. It took 3000 workmen one year to complete. Its official dimensions were 1880 feet long (more than six football fields) by 464 feet wide, and it was traversed by 11 miles of walkways. To see everything in the building would take an estimated two weeks, according to some who tried.

The cost of the Main Building was $1,580,000, paid for by the Centennial Board of Finance. The exterior of the building was painted light-brown with a red trim.

The building featured all types of commercial, industrial and international exhibits. The most significant item exhibited, although not necessarily thought to be so at the time, was Alexander Graham Bell's telephone.

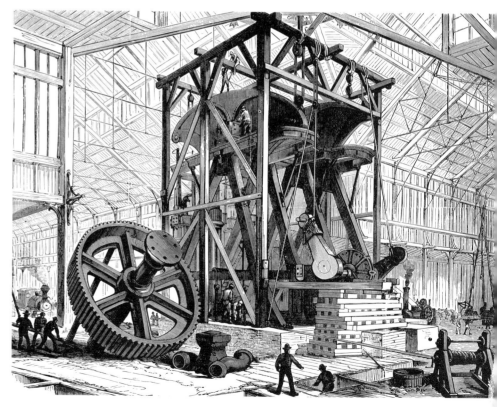

George H. Corliss (above) supplied the giant Corliss Engine (right and opposite page), which provided power for hundreds of other exhibits in Machinery Hall.

Second only to the Main Exhibition Hall in size was Machinery Hall, which stood on the same line with the Main Building and measured a mere 1402 feet in length (just short of five football fields) and 360 feet in width. The area covered by Machinery Hall and its annex boiler house was 13 acres.

All of the thousands of mechanical exhibits in Machinery Hall were driven by one large steam powered machine called the Corliss Engine in honor of its creator, New England industrialist George H. Corliss, whose participation in the Centennial was monumental in more ways than one. Twenty-three miles of shafting and 40 miles of belts helped propel everything in Machinery Hall. Cost of the building was $542,300. The cost of the Corliss Engine was $200,000, paid for by Corliss.

The Corliss engine was one of the highlights of the exhibition, and the fair remained closed on Sundays because of it. George Corliss was a devout churchgoer, and he strongly believed that Sunday should be a day of rest for everyone. Corliss' idea of rest did not include going to a fair. There was increasing pressure on the part of visitors to open the Centennial on Sundays, since that was the only day that most working Philadelphians could attend. The Centennial commissioners were about to give way until Corliss issued an ultimatum. Open on Sundays, he declared, and I'll take my engine and go home.

Corliss' threat worked, and the Centennial remained closed on Sundays.

Third in size of the buildings on the Centennial grounds was Agricultural Hall. It resembled a series of very ornate barn-like structures joined together for the exhibition of farm products, implements and livestock.

The United States in 1876 was already deep into the Industrial Revolution, and industry and agriculture were in competition at this first American world's fair. The official name of the Centennial Exhibition was "The International Exhibition of Arts, Manufactures and Products of the Soil and Mine," but most fairgoers never did learn the full name and simply called it "The Centennial."

Ranking behind these three large temporary exhibition halls in size were two slightly smaller permanent special exhibition buildings dedicated to art and horticulture.

Memorial Hall, which is the only major Centennial building still remaining today, was the fourth largest building and served as the International Art Gallery for the Centennial. It measures 365 feet in length and 210 feet in width, and features a double glass dome topped by a figure of Columbia. It is made of granite and glass and it was then, as it remains today, the landmark of the Centennial.

Most souvenirs of the Centennial pictured Memorial Hall. The building cost $1,500,000 and was paid for by the State of Pennsylvania and the City of Philadelphia.

Horticultural Hall, which remained as a horticultural exhibition center and a Fairmount Park attraction until it was demolished in 1955, was the fifth largest building on the Centennial grounds and one of the most ornate. It was 383 feet long and 193 feet wide and was constructed of iron

Workmen are placing the colossal figures depicting agriculture, commerce, industry and mining at the four corners of the base of the Memorial Hall dome (left). The U.S. Government Building was the largest of the many national buildings (above).

Aside from the five major buildings of the Centennial, two other large structures were the United States Government Building and the Women's Pavilion, located directly across from each other on Belmont Avenue, the main diagonal roadway of the fairgrounds.

The U. S. Government Building was by far the largest of the national buildings, and in overall dimensions was actually larger than both Memorial Hall and Horticultural Hall. The cost of the building was $110,000, paid for by the United States Government.

and glass. It housed botanical exhibits from around the world and featured many tropical plants never before seen by most Americans. The building cost $300,000, paid for by the City of Philadelphia.

THE
1776 United States 1876
CENTENNIAL INTERNATIONAL EXHIBITION

Shares 1.~   No. 91

THIS CERTIFIES THAT
is the holder of
of the Capital Stock of the Centennial Board of Finance incorporated by Act of Congress, approved June 1st 1872. Transferable only on the books of the Corporation on the surrender of this Certificate.

Witness the Seal of said Centennial Board of Finance at the City of Philadelphia this 21 day of April, 1875

Fred. Fraley.
Treasurer.
Shares $10. Each.

Ino. Welsh
President.
Capital $10.000.000.

Hermann J. Schwarzmann was the architectural genius behind the Centennial.

2

LET'S HAVE A PARTY

The idea for a major celebration in Philadelphia to commemorate the Centennial of American Independence apparently occurred to a number of people at about the same time.

Four people are noted as having "first" thought of a Centennial celebration for Philadelphia. John Bigelow, a former U. S. Minister to France; John L. Campbell, a professor at Wabash College in Indiana; M. Richards Muckle, a Philadelphia newspaper executive, and General Charles B. Norton, an American Commissioner at the Paris Exposition of 1867, each took credit for the plan.

The thought "occurred" to each of them in about 1866 when the nation reached its 90th birthday. For five or more years before that some might not have been willing to concede that the nation, as we knew it, would ever reach its 100th milestone.

If any one of the four Centennial visionaries could be singled out as the very first to call for a birthday party in Philadelphia, it might be John Campbell. In February, 1864, while the Civil War still raged, he spoke at the Smithsonian Institution on the 300th anniversary of the birth of Galileo, and the thought apparently occurred to him while delivering his address.

Campbell mulled over the idea for two years before sending his proposal to the Governor of Indiana and the

Foreign displays arriving in railroad cars are unloaded into the Main Building, passing first through the Customs House in the center foreground. No duties were imposed upon goods imported for the Centennial. The Judges' Pavilion is on the right.

Mayor of Philadelphia in 1866. Both were receptive to the idea, particularly Philadelphia Mayor Morton McMichael, who coincidentally became the first president of the new Fairmount Park Commission the following year.

McMichael apparently started the political mechanism in motion, and in March, 1870, a bill was introduced in Congress to celebrate the Centennial in Philadelphia in 1876.

Congressman Daniel J. Morrell, of Pennsylvania, introduced the bill on March 9, 1870, making provisions for the proposed exhibition. The bill was amended several times and finally adopted on March 3, 1871. It provided for the appointment by the President of a commissioner and an alternate from each state and territory, who were to be nominated by the governors of the states and territories. Philadelphia was selected as the site for the exhibition.

President Grant appointed most of the nominees during 1871. On March 4, 1872, one year and a day after the Act of Congress creating the Centennial, commissioners from 24 states and three territories and the District of Columbia met in Philadelphia.

Fittingly, John Campbell was appointed commissioner from Indiana, Congressman Morrell commissioner from Pennsylvania and George H. Corliss represented Rhode Island.

Joseph R. Hawley of Connecticut, a newspaper publisher, a retired Civil War general, and former governor and Congressman, was elected president of the commission. Professor Campbell was elected secretary, and his dream moved one step closer to reality. But the Centennial Commission was a widely diverse group, geographically and politically, and was in many cases saddled with political appointees with little or no real interest in the Philadelphia celebration.

In order to provide the necessary funds for the exhibition, and in a somewhat obvious effort to circumvent the unwieldy Centennial Commission, Congress on June 1, 1872, adopted a bill creating a "Centennial Board of Finance" with authorization to issue stock in shares of $10 each, the total amount of the issue not to exceed $10,000,000.

The members of the Board of Finance were appointed by the stockholders at a meeting in April, 1873. Most

The two halves of the Main Building are ready to be joined in front of the partially completed Memorial Hall (above). The finished Memorial Hall was an elegant structure (right).

were selected from Philadelphia to assure a quorum at all important votes. John Welsh, a prominent Philadelphia businessman, was elected chairman.

From the morass of 94 state and territorial Centennial commissioners and alternates, the Finance Board plucked a gem to serve as its Director-General. Alfred T. Goshorn, a Cincinnati lawyer and manufacturer, had gained invaluable experience as the supervisor of the annual Cincinnati Trade Fair. He and Welsh, with the aid of a handful of others, guided the Centennial through to triumph.

The Board of Finance was directed by its stockholders and Congress to begin at once the work of preparing the grounds and erecting the necessary buildings for the exhibition.

The Fairmount Park Commission, under the presidency of former Mayor McMichael, cooperated fully with the Centennial Commission, immediately offering 450 acres in West Fairmount Park.

The park land was formally turned over on loan to the Centennial Commission in appropriate ceremonies at the site on July 4, 1873. The ceremonies were opened with a prayer by Bishop Matthew Simpson, of the Methodist Episcopal Church, who would return on opening day in 1876 to offer up the opening prayer. Abraham Lincoln had sup-

posedly been hesitant about issuing the Emancipation Proclamation, and he reached his decision only after a long session of kneeling in prayer with Bishop Simpson at the White House.

Park Commission President McMichael turned the land officially over to Centennial Commission President Hawley, and concluded: "Who shall doubt that—stirred by memories of the turbulent past, urged by knowledge of the flourishing present, inspired by anticipation of the promising future—the people of the several States, and the States themselves in their sovereign capacities, as well as the Congress of the United States, will so assist your endeavors that in 1876 you will be enabled to present to the world a spectacle which, while typical of the skill and culture and ingenuity of the older nations, will conspicuously demonstrate what the thrift, intelligence, enterprise and energy of our own have achieved in a single century of existence."

Professor William P. Blake, alternate commissioner to President-Commissioner Hawley of Connecticut, who had edited the six-volume U. S. Report on the 1867 Paris Exposition, was sent along with others to the Vienna Exhibi-

tion in early 1873. He produced a detailed report calling for economical temporary structures and an effective mass transportation system for the Centennial.

Economic necessity dictated compliance with Blake's first point, and Pennsylvania Railroad President Thomas A. Scott saw to the latter with his masterful handling of Centennial transportation needs. Scott's efforts included the construction of the huge Pennsylvania Railroad Depot located directly opposite the Main Centennial Gate on Elm (now Parkside) Avenue, and the early installation of countless spur lines throughout the fairgrounds to facilitate delivery of construction materials. These construction lines remained and were concealed during the Centennial, to serve afterward in the dismantling of the buildings.

Meanwhile, a two-stage architectural competition for the design of the main buildings of the Centennial, launched on April 1, 1873, managed only to waste eight months of valuable time and $20,000 of valuable funds. The competition jury did decide, however, on the eventual plan of five major buildings: a main exhibition hall, a machinery hall, an agricultural hall, and a permanent art gallery and horticultural hall. It was also decided that the art gallery would remain in name and in fact as a Memorial Hall.

After returning from Vienna and while the abortive architectural competition was in progress, young Fairmount Park engineer Herman J. Schwarzmann worked up a complete survey of the 450 acres of Fairmount Park in the area of the Centennial site. He submitted his plan for the exhibition grounds, water supply and drainage on April 1, 1874, and it was immediately adopted.

Schwarzmann then set out to design the two permanent structures of the Centennial, Memorial Hall and Horticultural Hall. The Board of Finance on June 2, 1874, approved both of Schwarzmann's plans.

Schwarzmann was a remarkable fellow. Only 27 years old and a German immigrant, he was engineer of the Fairmount Park Commission in 1873. He became chief engineer for the Centennial in 1874, and ultimately designed 34 of the Centennial's buildings. Some of his other major buildings included the Judges' Pavilion, the Women's Pavilion, the Photography Exhibition Building, the Art Gallery Annex, the German Pavilion and the Pennsylvania Pavilion.

The huge Pennsylvania Railroad depot, located adjacent to the main entrance of the Centennial, was a temporary structure built to handle the thousands of visitors arriving by rail. It featured a large loop off of the main New York-Washington line of the Pennsy that permitted loading and unloading of passengers without turning around or switching.

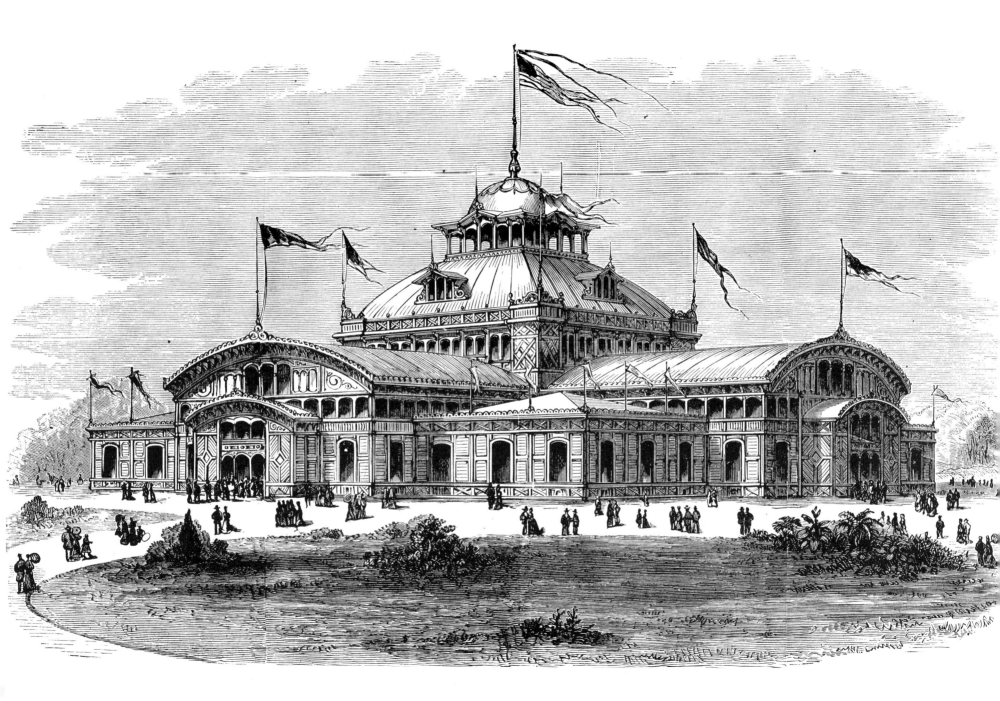

3

EVERY PARTY NEEDS A WOMAN'S TOUCH

Mrs. Elizabeth D. Gillespie (above) was the guiding light behind the Women's Pavilion (left) and was a major fund raiser for the Centennial.

One of the most popular buildings at the Centennial was the Women's Pavilion. Centrally located in the heart of the sprawling fairgrounds, the Women's Pavilion was a "must" stop for all female visitors to the Centennial.

A favorite practice of the day was for Dad to take the boys to Machinery Hall while Mom and the girls passed the time looking at the products and endeavors of women in the Women's Pavilion.

While President Grant and Emperor Dom Pedro pulled the levers that started the giant Corliss Engine in Machinery Hall, Mrs. Grant and Empress Theresa left their husbands to do similar honors at the Women's Pavilion, which featured its own engine house complete with a female engineer.

The Women's Pavilion, and perhaps the entire Centennial, was largely a tribute to the efforts of one woman: Mrs. Elizabeth D. Gillespie, the great-granddaughter of Benjamin Franklin.

Shortly after the Centennial Board of Finance conducted its first meeting in Philadelphia in April, 1873, the economy of the nation and the world fell into a deep depression. The Vienna Exhibition, conducted throughout the summer of 1873, was adversely affected by the sour economic climate, and the early efforts of the Centennial Board of Finance to sell stock went very poorly.

Mrs. Gillespie is seated at a table receiving reports at the Women's Centennial Committee Headquarters at 903 Walnut Street during the fund raising campaign prior to the Centennial (left). The Kindergarten Cottage, operated by the Women's Committee, instructed youngsters using the latest in pre-school teaching techniques (above).

The United States Government's contribution to date had been only $500,000, which was earmarked for constructing and furnishing the Government Building at the Centennial. The sale of stock was to be the main source of revenue. To help in the sale, the Board of Finance, comprised mostly of Philadelphia businessmen, turned to Philadelphia's women, and particularly to Mrs. Gillespie. Mrs. Gillespie accepted the challenge with vigor, and by the time the Centennial opened she had won the unofficial title of "Imperial Wizard of the Centennial."

Mrs. Gillespie traveled in Philadelphia's inner circle of movers and shakers, and personally combined the necessary Victorian attitude of the time with the strong belief in the rights of women. She firmly believed women should be able to participate in all facets of human endeavor hitherto reserved exclusively for men, and she saw the Centennial as a chance to further this goal.

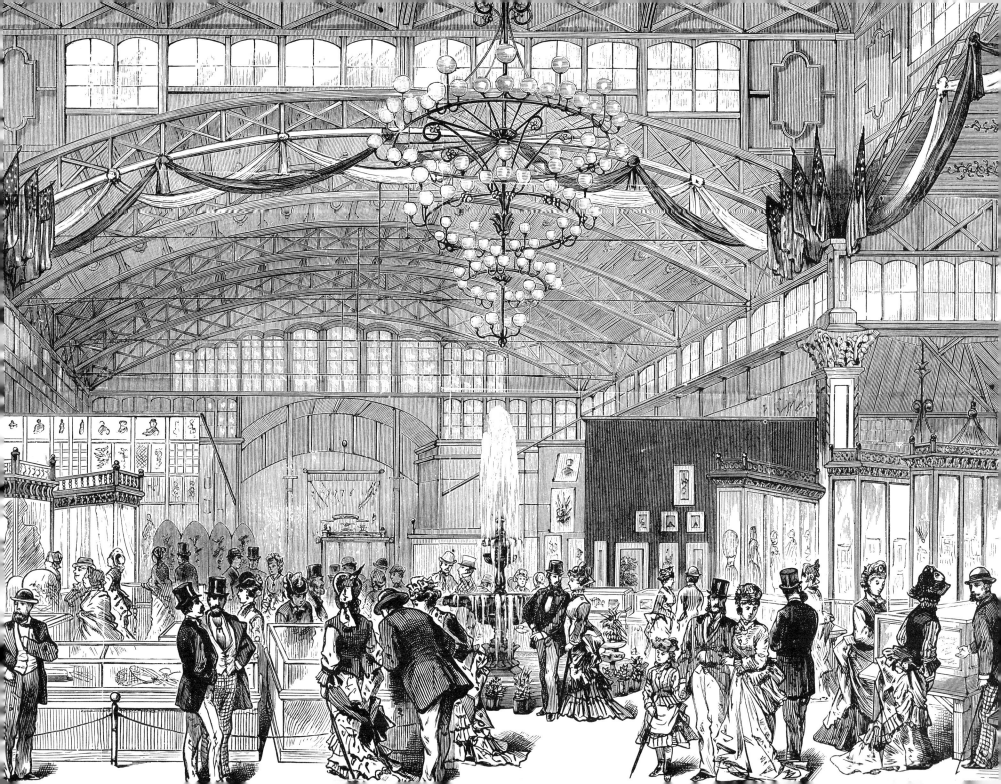

Through a city-wide, then nation-wide, series of committees, the women conducted teas, bazaars, concerts and art shows to sell Centennial stock. Despite the financial climate of 1873 and 1874, the women were able to raise in excess of $100,000, a figure that topped the contribution of every State except Pennsylvania and New York.

The driving force that kept Mrs. Gillespie and her associates going was the promise of space in the Main Exhibition Hall for a women's exhibit. But on June 11, 1875, Director-General Goshorn informed Mrs. Gillespie that due to the large number of other exhibitors reserving space, there would be no room in the Main Building for the women.

He suggested, half in jest, that perhaps the ladies would like to put up a building of their own on the Centennial grounds. Undaunted, Mrs. Gillespie and her committeewomen proceeded to raise an additional $30,000 to construct the Women's Pavilion. And they convinced Herman Schwarzmann to design it.

So discreetly had the incident of the separate Women's Pavilion and how it came about been handled by Mrs. Gillespie and her workers that many a male visitor to the Centennial was heard to ask: "Why do the women need a separate building? There's no men's pavilion. After all, aren't they talking about equal rights some day?"

The women even raised enough additional money to finance weekly symphony concerts and to sponsor a woman's magazine entitled "The New Century for Woman." The magazine was actually printed in the Women's Pavilion, and was "devoted to the industrial interests of women."

The year 1876 was a very important one in furthering the cause of women's rights. On the first day of the Centennial, the National Women's Suffrage Association also opened its meeting in New York City. Mrs. Gillespie was extremely sympathetic with the suffragette movement, but she was also wise enough to prevent it from being openly associated with the Women's Pavilion.

There is little doubt that Mrs. Gillespie played a behind-the-scenes role in the very interesting events that occurred at Independence Hall on July 4, 1876. At the official Centennial observance in front of Independence Hall, Susan B. Anthony and some of her suffragette supporters quietly

High-domed ceilings and hundreds of transom windows gave the Women's Pavilion an open and airy appearance (left). Displays in the building included the works and interests of women. To attain the height of fashion during the Centennial, ladies wore gowns which must have been unbearably hot and uncomfortable in the 90-degree weather (above).

marched onto the platform during the ceremonies and read their "Declaration of Independence for Women." The event received wide press coverage and helped to publicize the suffragette cause, even though another half century had to pass before women were allowed to vote in the national elections.

4

LET THE PARTY BEGIN

Opening day at the Centennial featured a sea of black umbrellas (left). Small boys were enraptured by the uniforms of foreign military officers who visited the fair (above).

The party of the century had a guest list befitting the occasion of the nation's 100th birthday and the first world's fair in the Americas. Invitations from President Grant were to go out to the governors of all 37 states, 10 territories and the District of Columbia, and to the kings, queens, emperors, potentates and other rulers of every nation in the world, inviting them to participate in the Centennial.

The sending of the invitations, however, was no simple matter. There were some in Congress and elsewhere who, for various reasons, challenged the President's right to invite foreign nations to participate. Strongest in his opposition to the hosting of an international exhibition in Philadelphia was Massachusetts' abolitionist Senator Charles Sumner.

Sumner and the Congressional bloc he headed not only delayed legislation to fund the exhibition, but through influence wielded within the President's own cabinet initiated a State Department circular that went out early in 1872 advising American diplomats abroad that "the President has extended no invitation to foreign powers to participate. He was not authorized to do so."

As valuable time slipped by, there was nothing Philadelphia's Centennial planners could do but attempt to raise money through the sale of stock, encourage international participation by whatever means possible and prepare

THIS SHOVEL
WAS USED IN OPENING THE GROUND IN
FAIRMOUNT PARK
For the Foundations
OF THE
CENTENNIAL BUILDINGS,
on the Fourth day of July, A.D. 1874.
BY THE HON.
WILLIAM S. STOKLEY
MAYOR
OF THE
CITY OF PHILADELPHIA

the site as prescribed by the initial federal legislation.

A pall fell over the Centennial. Added to the gloom from Washington was the bleak word from Vienna. Things were not going well there, as some of the Centennial planners were learning first hand.

The official and unofficial U. S. and Philadelphia delegations to the International Exhibition in Vienna in 1873 found it "a mess." Visitors were staying away in droves, most of the exhibition was incomplete because of foul-ups at European ports, the first rumblings of the depression of '73 had already closed the Vienna Bourse and a cholera epidemic threatened the city.

The Centennial planners returned from Vienna discouraged, but with a resolve not to let the problems of Vienna become problems in Philadelphia. To further compound the bad news, as the delegates prepared to leave Vienna they received word that the Philadelphia banking house of Jay Cooke had folded because of the growing worldwide depression.

Amidst all the bad news, word came from Washington that Senator Sumner had died suddenly of apoplexy. Centennial officials were openly joyful.

Congress still wasn't ready to fund the Centennial, but it did soften its stand on international participation and authorized the President to invite foreign nations to take part in 1876. On June 5, 1874, Grant signed the bill officially inviting foreign nations to participate.

On the Fourth of July, 1874, ground was broken in Fairmount Park for the Centennial with appropriate ceremonies. The day was one of the biggest in memory in Philadelphia. Aside from the very large and enthusiastic crowds at the Centennial groundbreaking and the traditional Independence Hall ceremony, large crowds also attended the formal opening of the Girard Avenue Bridge across the Schuylkill River, and the cornerstone laying ceremony of the new Philadelphia City Hall on Center Square at Broad and Market Streets. The Girard Avenue Bridge would serve as the major access route to the Centennial and City Hall was to become a Victorian architectural landmark.

The next day, July 5, Secretary of State Hamilton Fish forwarded President Grant's Centennial Proclamation to the various ministers of foreign countries residing in the na-

Centennial officials invited President Grant and all members of Congress to a banquet in the partially completed Horticultural Hall on December 20, 1875, in a successful attempt to raise money (above). The Congressmen went back to Washington and promptly approved another $1,500,000 to complete the Centennial. The shovel used in the groundbreaking ceremonies on July 4, 1874, was on display during the fair (left).

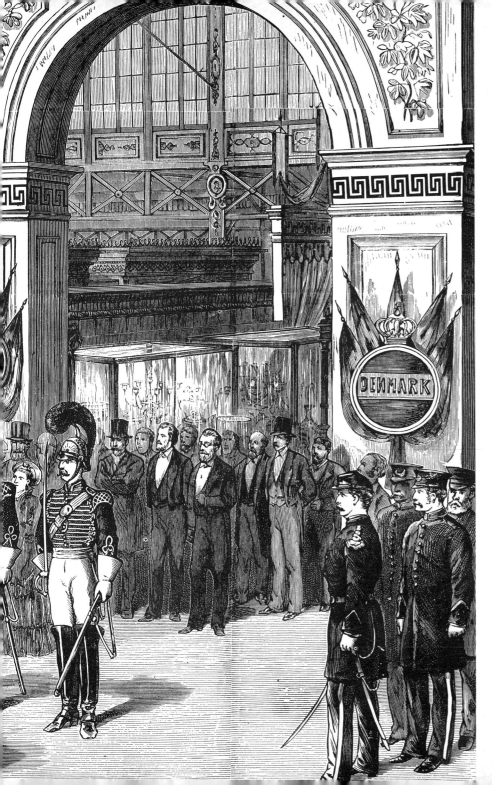

Brazilian Emperor Dom Pedro stole the spotlight at the opening ceremonies (above). President Grant and Dom Pedro are introduced to the various foreign commissioners in the Main Exhibition Building on opening day (left).

President Grant viewed the exhibits in Memorial Hall prior to the opening ceremonies (left). Later he and Dom Pedro started the giant Corliss Engine in Machinery Hall (right).

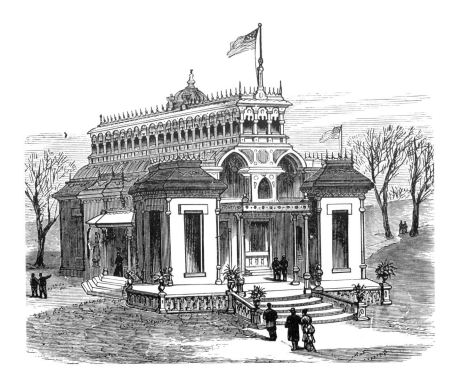

The various state buildings were a conglomeration of architectural styles. The Michigan Building (above) seems to drip with Victorian gingerbread. The Massachusetts Building (top left) resembles a barn, and the Indiana Building looked like a mausoleum (bottom left). The Arkansas Building looked like a carrousel (top right), the Iowa (bottom right) and Illinois buildings (far top right) resembled homes, and the Kansas Building (far bottom right) could have been a railroad station.

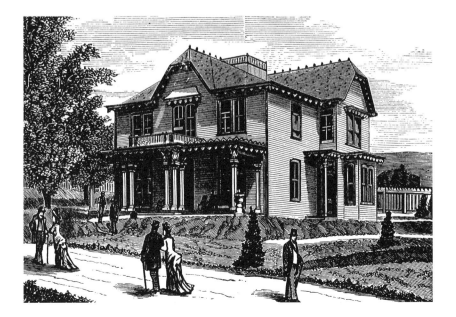

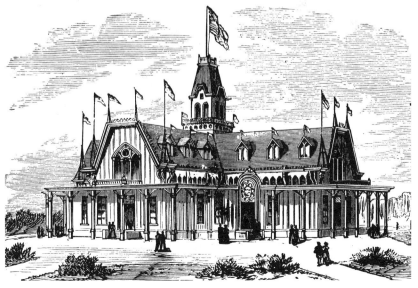

Foreign buildings included the
Brazilian Pavilion (left), the Por-
tuguese Pavilion (far top left) and the
German Empire Pavilion (above).
Japanese workmen operate a primitive pile-driving device in laying the
foundation of the Japanese Building
(right).

Turkish carpenters are just beginning work on the Turkish Bazaar (above),
which proved an extremely popular exhibit with fairgoers. Visitors to the
completed Turkish Bazaar are very comfortably smoking what is apparently something stronger than tobacco (right).

48

state Pennsylvania and nearby New York and New Jersey. Apparently none of the state buildings proved very distinguished from an architectural viewpoint, at least according to most reports. One architectural magazine of the time reported that it was anticipated with "dread" that the state buildings would be given to the city and the park after the Centennial.

Distinguished above the others perhaps was the Ohio House, which stood as the first in the line of 16 state buildings along States Drive stretching from Belmont Avenue to the foot of George's Hill. The Ohio Building was constructed of native Ohio stone from 21 different quarries. (The Ohio House is the only Centennial building except for Memorial Hall and some minor outbuildings of Horticultural Hall still standing in Fairmount Park.)

In addition to the regular state buildings, Pennsylvania erected a separate Pennsylvania Education Building located adjacent to Memorial Hall. And Tennessee and Virginia were unofficially represented, Tennessee with a tent situated between the Maryland and Iowa buildings and Virginia with a small guest house located behind the Wo

men's Pavilion. The Tennessee and Virginia facilities were erected by private individuals.

*   *   *

The story of opening day at the Centennial has been told perhaps as often as any other single non-tragic event in American history. The day was one of national exaltation laced with prophetic international overtones.

President Grant was quite naturally the guest of honor and delivered the official opening address. But the ex-war hero's popularity was waning fast as he neared the end of his eight-year administration. After early rumors of a third term, the Grant Administration was wracked with scandal at the highest cabinet level. Bribery charges against Secretary of War William Belknap and the "Whiskey Ring" scandal in the Treasury Department had killed all talk of a third term.

It was a decidedly subdued, somewhat besmirched President who came to Philadelphia to officially open the Centennial on May 10, 1876. It was an easy matter for the colorful Brazilian Emperor Dom Pedro and his charm

Methods for moving blocks of stone and trees were primitive by today's standards (left). An exhibit that attracted much attention was an outdoor scale model of the city of Paris (above).

ing wife to steal the limelight throughout what should have been an all-American day.

The official ceremonies took place on a large temporary platform erected in front of Memorial Hall. It had rained the day before and was still raining at 9 A.M. when the Centennial gates opened for the first time for paying customers.

The exact change requirement (a 50-cent note) combined with the crush at the 179 new-fangled, self-registering turnstiles infuriated the impatient crowds at every entrance, many of whom had been waiting in the rain for hours. Large numbers (estimated by some at 100,000 or more) did not pay, but jumped the fences or went through the turnstiles two and three at a time. Another large number of gate crashers swarmed in with the official procession of 4000 dignitaries through a special gate. Official attendance sheets for the day recorded 76,172 paid admissions, but unofficial estimates pegged the attendance for the day at 200,000 or more. It was believed by everyone to be the largest civilian crowd ever assembled in the history of the United States.

The throng gathered in front of Memorial Hall for the official opening was estimated at 100,000.

Aside from the very large platform that had been erected on the front steps of Memorial Hall for dignitaries and guests, another large bleacher-type scaffolding stood across the Avenue of the Republic (now North Concourse) at the side entrance to the Main Exhibition Building.

The ceremony was scheduled for 10 A.M. Emperor Dom Pedro and Empress Theresa arrived first and were instantly recognized by the crowd from newspaper acounts of their pending opening day visit and earlier visits to New York City and Washington.

While the crowd cheered the Brazilian royal visitors, the official parade arrived and pandemonium broke loose as spectators scurried to avoid the oncoming cavalry escort. Confusion reigned as the President and First Lady made their appearance almost unnoticed. A handkerchief was waved frantically from the platform, and the orchestra struck up "Hail to the Chief."

After the President and the First Lady were seated on the platform, the orchestra performed the premiere performance of the "Centennial March," composed especially for the occasion by Richard Wagner at the cost of

The world's first monorail railway spanned a small ravine in Fairmount Park during the Centennial (top left). A ride on the 500-foot line took two minutes and cost three cents. Inside the car were two levels for passengers (left). The "broom brigade" kept the fairgrounds free of litter (above).

Two observation towers at the Centennial featured different types of elevators (right).

$5000, paid for by Mrs. Gillespie's Women's Centennial Committee.

Centennial Commission President Hawley introduced the Reverend Simpson, who delivered what everyone agreed was an overly long prayer. More music followed.

Finally, the moment came to introduce the President. Hawley first presented a brief history of the Centennial project, then turned to Grant and said, "I present to your view the International Exhibition of 1876."

After a brief burst of applause and some small commotion in the audience, the President spoke:

"One hundred years ago our country was new and but partially settled. Our necessities have compelled us chiefly to expend our means and time in felling forests, subduing prairies, building dwellings, factories, ships, docks, warehouses, roads, canals, machinery, etc. Most of our schools, churches, libraries, and asylums have been established within a hundred years. Burdened by these great primal works of necessity, which could not be delayed, we have yet done what this Exhibition will show in the direction of rivaling older and more advanced nations in law, medicine and theology, in science, literature, philosophy and the fine arts. Whilst proud of what we have done, we regret that we have not done more. Our achievements have been great enough, however, to make it easy for our people to acknowledge superior merit wherever found."

Thus, in a paragon of brevity and understatement, uninterrupted by applause and mostly unheard even by those on the platform, the eighteenth President of the United States officially opened the nation's 100th birthday party.

The President and the Emperor and their wives then proceeded through the Main Exhibition Building to Machinery Hall to activate the great Corliss Engine. Since it wasn't a Sunday, Corliss was on hand in person to direct the two world leaders in the turning of two separate levers provided for the occasion. The crowd gasped as first Grant and then Dom Pedro turned the levers and the 700-ton monster spit some steam and began to revolve. In turn, hundreds of other machines through the buildings began to hum and operate. Everyone seemed delighted. Even the dour Grant smiled.

And the giant birthday party had begun.

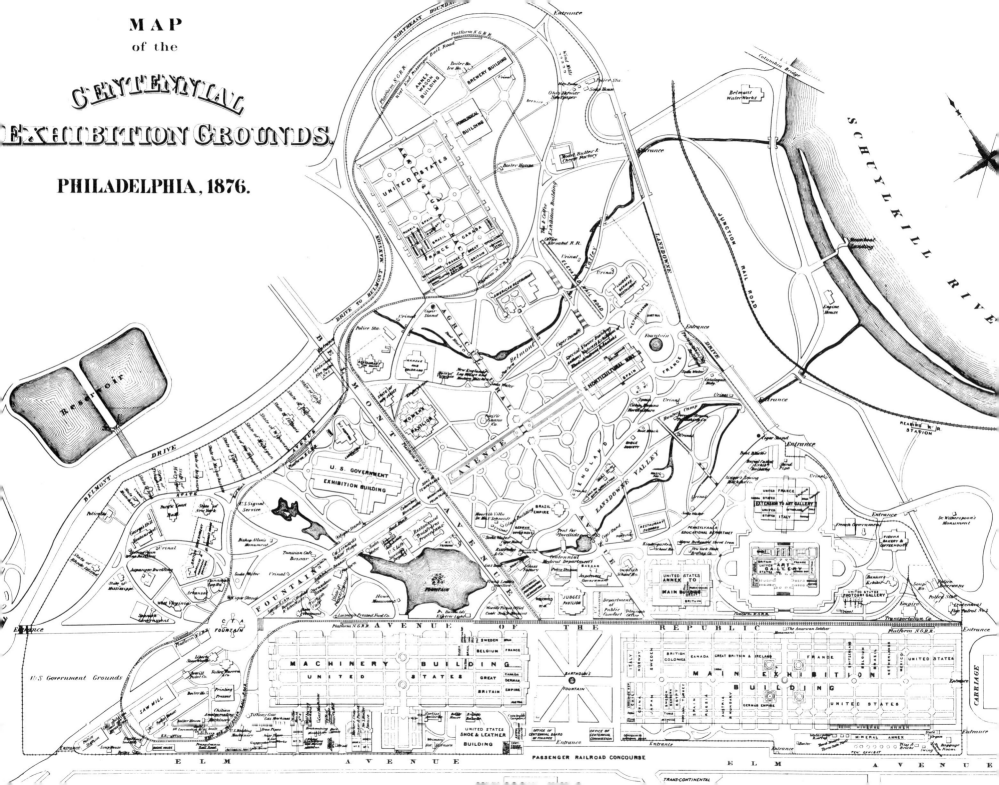

5

PARTY GAMES AND ENTERTAINMENT

Unpacking statues before the fair opened.

Although the Centennial was intended to be a patriotic showing of the accomplishments of a proud, young nation, most of the nearly 10 million visitors came to be entertained. And entertained they were.

From opening day, when the visiting Brazilians stole the spotlight from the Grants, until closing day when President Grant returned alone to bring down the curtain on the party of the century, Centennial visitors were entertained for 159 straight days (not including Sundays).

Each morning thousands of persons waited in lines at the 179 turnstile entrances for the 9 A.M. opening. Once inside the gates, those who had bought their program books and catalogs in advance or those who had been briefed by friends and relatives after earlier visits to the fair, hurried to beat the crowds to the most popular attractions.

The 40-foot high Corliss Engine in Machinery Hall was a most popular exhibit for men and boys, particularly the first thing in the morning when the "sleeping giant" was turned on and the mammoth 30-foot flywheel lumbered quietly and effortlessly into motion, activating hundreds of other machines through an intricate series of belts and wheels strung throughout the massive building.

Others rushed to Agricultural Hall to get a close look at the battle scarred war eagle "Old Abe." The aging mascot of the Eighth Wisconsin Regiment was said to have

The view down Belmont Avenue, the main midway (left). Independence Hall was ablaze with fireworks during the mammoth Fourth of July celebration (right).

The 21-acre Main Building contained 12,000 exhibits and 11 miles of aisles and walkways (above). A bandstand in the center of the building was the scene of regular concerts that attracted thousands (right).

Philadelphia's Baldwin Locomotive Works proudly displayed several shiny steam engines in Machinery Hall (left). The Corliss Engine is in the background. Agricultural Hall featured some giant German wine bottles (right).

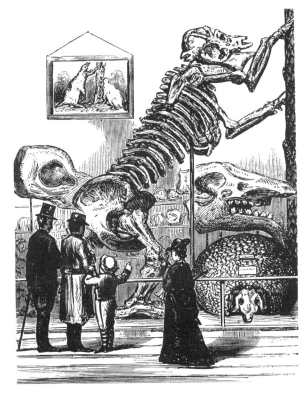

Dinosaur skeletons fascinated young visitors (above).

Dominating the interior of Machinery Hall were two Krupp cannon from Germany.

Lake across from Machinery Hall. It stood about 40 feet in height and one or two people could wriggle up inside the arm to walk around the base of the gas lighted torch, which was said to be able to hold a dozen people at one time. Few who saw it could believe that a statue of such gigantic proportions could ever be built.

After the Centennial closed, the arm was transported to New York City where it was placed on display in Madison Square and served as a fund raising symbol. It was 1889 before this project was completed on Bedloe's Island.

Second only to Bartholdi's Light in size of all the statues on the Centennial grounds was the 21-foot tall white stone figure of "The American Volunteer." It stood just outside the north entrance of the Main Exhibition Hall on a 15-foot pedestal. It depicted a Civil War soldier leaning on his rifle, and was one of the few and by far the largest reminder of the Civil War at the Centennial. It was made by the American Granite Company of Hartford, Connecticut, and was the work of company employee Carl Conrads, a Bavarian-born stonecutter.

The B'nai B'rith had Moses Ezekiel, the first Jewish-American sculptor, create a work called "Religious Liberty," which was prominently located on the axis of the sunken gardens leading from the Catholic Fountain to Horticultural Hall.

Late in the Centennial year the Italian Societies of the United States unveiled the Christopher Columbus statue located just opposite the B'nai B'rith statue on Belmont Avenue. The marble statue was by an unknown Italian artist and was officially dedicated on Columbus Day, less than a month before the Centennial closed.

Almost every one of the 159 days of the Centennial Exhibition was a special day. The state days, celebrated mostly toward the end of the fair, were by far the most successful from an attendance standpoint.

Some other special days included the opening of the International Billiard Tournament in Horticultural Hall on May 15, the dedication of the Ice Water Temperance Fountain by the National Division of the Sons of Temperance on June 15 (it is often mistakenly reported that ice was put in the Catholic Fountain for cool drinks at the Centennial), the opening of the Ten Days' Encampment of the West Point

Cadets on June 30, the opening of the International Rowing Regatta on the Schuylkill River adjacent to the Centennial grounds on August 22, the opening of the Live-Stock Displays for Horses, Mules and Asses in Agricultural Hall on September 1, and other less thrilling events, most of which were highly successful.

The Fourth of July, which might have been expected to be the biggest day of all at the Centennial, was not. The Centennial Commission had decided early in the year that since the Declaration of Independence was ratified on the Fourth of July 100 years before at Independence Hall, the Centennial Fourth of July celebration should be there and not on the Centennial grounds.

The Fourth dawned oppressively hot, and in order to beat the heat the 10,000 marching troops formed at 7 A.M. and marched off down Chestnut Street toward Independence Hall at 8:30.

The Emperor of Brazil once again stole the spotlight at Independence Hall on the Fourth of July, as he had on opening day at the Centennial. This time the theft was complete, since President Grant declined the invitation to attend, sending instead Vice President Thomas W. Ferry.

Nude sculpture and paintings from Italy and France found an enthusiastically receptive audience in Victorian America (far left). One of the more popular works was "Love Blinds," by Italian Donato Barcaglia (left). A spectacular fire destroyed Shantyville just outside the Centennial grounds, threatening for a time the Main Building (above).

Black visitors to Memorial Hall admired the symbolic statue of "The Freed Slave" (right). The interior of Memorial Hall featured many of the 325 pieces of sculpture sent from Italy for the Contonnial (left).

One contemporary account said that Grant "remained in Washington, preferring his selfish ease to a little patriotic exertion and exposure to the heat on this grandest of his country's festivals. His absence was generally remarked and severely condemned by his countrymen."

The ceremonies at Independence Hall were presided over by General Hawley, president of the Centennial Commission. Poet Bayard Taylor and orator William M. Evarts were the featured speakers. Among the other guests were William Tecumseh Sherman, commanding general of the U.S. Army; Prince Oscar, secretary of war for Sweden; Lt. Gen. Saigi, of the Imperial Army of Japan; John F. Hartranft, governor of Pennsylvania, and John Welsh, chairman of the Centennial Board of Finance. The ceremony began at 10 A.M. and was over well before noon. The crowd was large and enthusiastic, despite the heat.

However, the real crowd had been there the night before when an estimated 100,000 marched in a torchlight parade to Independence Square to watch the clock in Independence Hall tower reach midnight of the Fourth of July, 1876, and to hear the "new" liberty bell in the steeple toll 13 times.

Out at the Centennial grounds on the Fourth, the Catholic Total Abstinence Society dedicated the Catholic Fountain and the German-American Society dedicated the statue of Alexander von Humboldt. Attendance for the day exceeded 47,000.

The biggest day of the entire Centennial celebration occurred on Thursday, September 28, when well over a quarter of a million people (257,169 paid, 274,919 total) came to the fair to take part in "Pennsylvania Day." It was the largest single crowd ever to attend a world's fair anywhere.

The largest official crowd up until that time had been 173,923 that had attended the Paris Exhibition on October 27, 1867. The opening day crowd at the Centennial on May 10 had probably also topped the Paris record, but only 76,172 were officially recorded.

"Pennsylvania Day" was the 200th anniversary of the adoption of the first Constitution of Pennsylvania, and Governor Hartranft had declared a legal holiday throughout the state. Businesses throughout Philadelphia were closed and thousands arrived early at the fairgrounds. The gates

were opened 30 minutes early at 8:30 A.M. By 10 A.M., a check of the automatic tabulating turnstiles showed that 175,000 people had already entered the fairgrounds, and they were still coming.

Special entertainment was planned throughout the day, including concerts and music recitals in the Main Building. The various exhibitors of musical instruments offered performances at their respective stands, and the chimes of Machinery Hall rang forth with patriotic and other melodies throughout the day.

Governor Hartranft, of course, was the guest of honor, and receptions were held throughout the day at the Pennsylvania Building, at the Judges' Hall sponsored by the Women's Centennial Committee and at the Philadelphia Building, near Horticultural Hall, hosted by Mayor William S. Stokley.

At nightfall an estimated 175,000 gathered within the fairgrounds near George's Hill and a like number outside for a grand finale fireworks display by Brock and Company, of London. It was long after midnight before the railroad and carriage depots and streets around the Exhibition grounds were cleared of the largest crowd in the history of world's fairs.

"New Jersey Day" on August 24, "Connecticut Day" on September 7, "Massachusetts Day" on September 14, "New York Day" on September 21, "Rhode Island Day" on October 5, "New Hampshire Day" combined with "Italian Day" on October 12 and "Ohio Day" on October 26 were all similar to "Pennsylvania Day," with varying degrees of success.

Only "Delaware-Maryland-Virginia Day" on October 19 was different. The state government of Virginia declined to take part, so officially it became "Delaware-Maryland Day," although a large number of Virginians participated. The 176,407 grand total attendance for the day ranked it second only to "Pennsylvania Day," and it, too, topped the previous single day high achieved at the Paris Exhibition in 1867. Highlight of the day was a jousting tournament, in which 15 men dressed as knights on horseback (representing the 13 original states, the Union and the Centennial) entertained 60,000 spectators.

Not all of the entertainment was within the fairgrounds.

"The American Volunteer" was one of the few reminders of the recent Civil War (left). Known as Bartholdi's Light, the arm of the Statue of Liberty was first exhibited at the Centennial (right). A dozen visitors at a time could walk around the base of the lamp.

CONGRESS SHALL MAKE NO LAW
RESPECTING AN ESTABLISHMENT OF RELIGION
OR PROHIBITING THE FREE EXERCISE THEREOF

U.S. Constitution

The statue of "Religious Liberty" was placed by B'nai B'rith at the end of the sunken gardens near Horticultural Hall (far left). Imaginative parents found many ways to entertain small children at the Centennial (left).

Delaware-Maryland-Virginia Day on October 19 featured a jousting tournament with mounted "knights" (below).

The entire fairgrounds was jammed with visitors as attendance reached
275,000 on Pennsylvania Day on September 28.

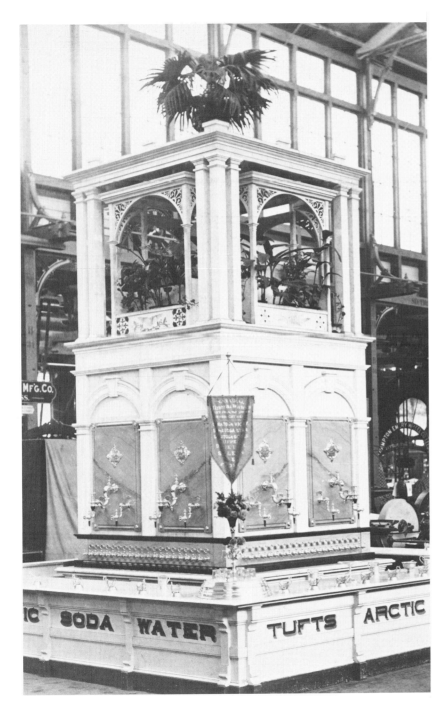

Hires Root Beer was introduced at the Centennial, but the Tufts Arctic Soda Water Company was the chief beverage concessionaire with numerous stands located throughout the fairgrounds (left). Waffles and popcorn were also very popular (above). The Brazilian Cafe offered light snacks and specialized in—naturally—home-grown coffee (below). The picturesque fountains and botanic exhibits of Horticultural Hall were a pleasant relief from the bustling crowds (opposite page).

Resting spots for weary sightseers were available in the Public Comfort Building (above), as was a popular oyster bar (right). The Dairy was a favorite open-air restaurant (top right).

78

Shantyville, or "Dinkertown," which had sprung up across Elm Avenue, was a popular attraction for men and boys. Can-can dancers, the wild man of Borneo and a fat lady who broke a chair by sitting on it were among the midway offerings. On September 9, the four-acre Shantyville burned in a spectacular fire that for a while threatened the Main Exhibition Building.

Like all tourists, Centennial visitors scheduled their day's touring around their meals and where they were going to eat. The Centennial was specifically planned with this in mind, and the Department of Public Comfort Building, located just off the main plaza next to the Judge's Pavilion, was the best attempt at any world's fair yet held to provide for visitors' comforts, including food.

The Public Comfort Building (right) included public toilets, a lost and found, post office and telegraph facilities and several restaurants (below).

Rest rooms, writing rooms, a parcel check, lost and found, informal meeting areas and quick food service facilities helped meet all the needs of Centennial visitors under one roof. More than 300 employees staffed the lunch counters and restaurants in the Public Comfort Building.

Aside from the numerous small lunch counters and restaurants located in the Public Comfort Building and throughout the fairgrounds, there were seven large first-class restaurants on the Centennial grounds.

The largest and most handsome was the Grand American Restaurant, located just south of Agricultural Hall and not far from Horticultural Hall. It was 200 by 300 feet in size and was built around three sides of a court opening to the south. Five thousand diners could be seated at one time.

The Southern Restaurant was situated just north of the Women's Pavilion on Belmont Avenue and had four large dining rooms and 16 private rooms for parties. As its name suggested, it served specialty dishes from the South and catered to visitors from the Southern states. It could accommodate 1000 guests.

There were two French restaurants at the Centennial.

The Restaurant of the Trois Freres Provenceaux (Three Brothers of Provence) was located on the west side of Belmont Avenue on the north shore of Centennial Lake and just to the south of the Government Building. Seating 1000 people, it was a duplicate of the restaurant of the same name in Paris and was under the same management as the famous Paris restaurant.

Not only was Trois Freres the classiest restaurant on the Centennial grounds, it was also the most expensive. Diners were charged separately for bread, butter and service, a standard French custom but an outrage to many Americans. The standing joke at the Centennial was that when you ate there you received separate bills from each of the three brothers.

The Restaurant Lafayette was the other French dining spot. It was a handsome two-story frame structure located on the south slope of Lansdowne Ravine not far from Memorial Hall. The second floor offered open air dining with a good view of the nearby pavilions. It was one of the most attractive of the eating establishments at the fair, and seated 1000 persons.

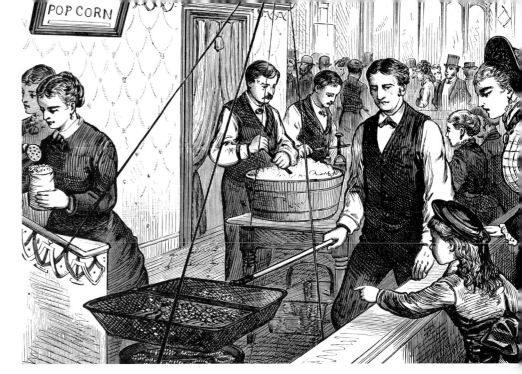

Coffee was served in the Turkish Bazaar (below), while visitors to the Tunisian Cafe could drink tea and enjoy the "scarf dancer," a naughty young lady who actually went so far as to bare her ankles to fascinated spectators (left). Popcorn was a new and popular snack at the Centennial (right). In Shantyville, across the street from the Centennial, it was reported that ladies of the evening sold popcorn on the streets as a come-on for other business transactions.

The German Restaurant, or, as it was better known, Lauber's Restaurant, was situated just northeast of Horticultural Hall. Lauber's was operated by an enterprising Philadelphian named Philip J. Lauber, and the 1200-seat establishment was the most successful and popular at the Centennial.

The Vienna Bakery and Cafe Fleischmann was a tasteful wood structure at the eastern end of the fairgrounds near the Reading Railroad Depot entrance to the Centennial. It featured a bakery where fresh bread was constantly baked and served in a coffee house adjoining the bakery.

George's Hill Restaurant was a frame building located near the western end of the row of state buildings at the foot of George's Hill. It was also called the Hebrew Restaurant because it catered to the desires of Jewish visitors.

Just to the southwest of George's Hill Restaurant was a small pavilion that sold the wines and liquors of Hungary, served by attendants in Hungarian dress.

The Dairy was a partially open-air, rustic log structure on the northern slope of Lansdowne Ravine opposite Horticultural Hall. It was operated by an association of dairymen in Philadelphia, and it specialized in fresh milk, cream, buttermilk and ice cream.

The Tea and Coffee Press Building was an attractive structure with a tower at each end. Its main purpose was to demonstrate and sell tea and coffee "presses," new devices for the preparation of these drinks. The drinks were sold at small cost, and were usually served over ice throughout the hot Centennial summer.

All in all, the culinary needs of Centennial visitors were well served.

6 🏵

EVERY PARTY HAS ITS LATECOMERS

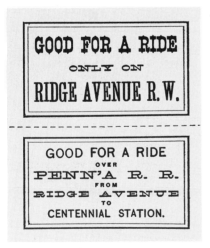

The evening rush hour was a chaotic time at the horsecar terminal next to the Pennsylvania Railroad depot (left). A two-part ticket was good for a ride on the horsecar and on the Pennsy (above).

Many have referred to the period of the world's fair of 1876 in Philadelphia as the "Centennial Summer." But a look at the attendance figures quickly indicates that for most visitors it was a "Centennial Autumn."

After an unofficial attendance of 200,000 (79,172 paid) on opening day, Centennial officials geared up to handle the throngs. More ticket takers and turnstile operators were hired for the 13 entrances and 179 turnstiles.

But the throngs didn't come.

On the second day of the Centennial only 14,722 visitors showed up. The third day dropped to 10,252, and by May 16 attendance was down to 7,056.

Attendance perked up slightly throughout the rest of the month, with the highest attendance of 41,111 recorded on May 30. The average daily attendance through May was 20,000. During the month of June attendance increased slightly, with the highest single day's attendance at 39,386 and the lowest at 20,343. The daily average attendance in June was just under 27,000.

The period around the Fourth of July, which was extremely hot in Philadelphia, saw attendance rise to 47,786 on the 3rd, 46,290 on the 4th, 51,825 on the 5th and 46,088 on the 6th. Attendance fell off rapidly after the 6th, and by July 30 it was down to only 15,207. The daily average in July was only 24,000.

ATTENDANCE BY MONTH

Month	Days	Paid Admissions	Total Admissions
May	19	378,980	613,495*
June	26	695,666	952,177
July	26	636,518	906,447
August	27	908,684	1,175,314
September	26	2,130,991	2,439,689
October	26	2,334,530	2,663,879
November	9	918,956	1,038,391
	159	8,004,325	9,789,392

*Includes estimated 110,500 free admissions on opening day

COMPARISON WITH PREVIOUS WORLD'S FAIRS

Year	Place	Days	Total Attendance	Receipts
1851	London	141	6,039,195	$2,120,000.
1855	Paris	200	5,162,330	$ 640,497.
1862	London	171	6,211,103	$2,044,650.
1867	Paris	210	8,806,969	$2,103,675.
1873	Vienna	186	7,254,687	$1,032,090.
1876	Philadelphia	159	9,789,392	$3,813,749.

LARGEST SINGLE ATTENDANCE DAYS

Philadelphia, 1876	257,286	Thursday, September 28, 1876
Paris, 1867	173,923	Sunday, October 27, 1867
Vienna, 1873	135,674	Sunday, November 2, 1873
Paris, 1855	123,017	Sunday, September 9, 1855
London, 1851	109,915	Tuesday, October 7, 1851
London, 1862	67,891	Thursday, October 30, 1862

(Note that Sundays were the most popular days at Paris and Vienna, but the Centennial was closed on Sundays.)

Many fairgoers got their first glimpse of the Centennial from a Pennsylvania Railroad train crossing the Girard Avenue Bridge (opposite page). Hotel accommodations were sometimes scarce, and would-be guests fought hard to get a room (right).

ATTENDANCE ON STATE DAYS

	Paid	Total
New Jersey Day, August 24	56,325	67,052
Connecticut Day, September 7	64,059	75,044
Massachusetts Day, September 14	85,795	97,868
New York Day, September 21	122,003	134,588
Pennsylvania Day, September 28	257,169	274,919
Rhode Island Day, October 5	89,060	100,946
New Hampshire Day, October 12	101,541	118,422
Delaware-Maryland Day, October 19	161,355	176,407
Ohio Day, October 26	122,300	135,661

The heat wave that began late in June continued through August, and the fairgrounds and Centennial buildings were uncomfortably hot and steamy. But August was traditionally vacation month, and as they were beginning to say across the country: "You only get one chance in a lifetime to visit a Centennial." Led by the 50,209 people who attended on "New Jersey Day" on the 24th, August's daily attendance jumped up to nearly 34,000.

Apparently the August and earlier summer crowds, small though they had been, had spread the word about the glories of the Centennial, and attendance skyrocketed throughout September, October and early November.

Despite the fact that children had to go back to school and the peak vacation period was over, September finally brought the throngs which had been expected earlier. On the 1st, 34,182 attended; on the 5th, 50,209; and except for one rainy day later in the season, attendance never fell below 50,000 a day throughout the rest of the Centennial. September 7 was "Connecticut Day," and attendance was 04,059, the 14th was "Massachusetts Day" with 85,705 attending; the 21st was "New York Day" and 122,003 arrived for the largest official attendance to date. The day before, the 20th, attendance reached the 100,000 paid mark for the first time when 101,498 paid admissions were recorded.

Then on September 28, "Pennsylvania Day," the largest single crowd of the entire Centennial came to the fair with 257,169 paid admissions recorded and total attendance reaching 274,919. The daily average for September was an astounding 82,000.

The beautiful autumn days of October brought out even more people, and attendance continued to soar. The very lowest day of the month still had 65,865 visitors, and "Delaware-Maryland Day" on the 19th was tops for the month with 161,355. Average daily attendance in October was 90,000.

Visitors in the last 10 days of the fair, November 1 through November 10, averaged 92,000, with attendance topping the 100,000 mark on four of the 10 days. On November 9, the next to the last day, attendance reached 176,755, the second highest daily total. On closing day, 106,474 people paid their way into the fairgrounds for a final look at the wonder of the century.

New York Day on September 21 featured a parade of New York City policemen (left). New York Governor Samuel J. Tilden reviewed the troops from the roof of the New York Building. The horsecar and railroad companies were often hard-pressed to carry everybody who wanted to go to the Centennial (above and below).

The terra cotta fountain "Out in the Rain" was one of many charming pieces of Italian sculpture at the Centennial (above). The umbrellas were up again on closing day (left).

7

THE PARTY'S OVER

Closing day of the Centennial, November 10, like opening day six months earlier, came up wet. The outdoor ceremony planned for the central plaza of the fairgrounds between the Main Building and Machinery Hall near the Bartholdi Fountain was cancelled in favor of the drier confines of the Judges' Pavilion.

President Grant, still smarting from the public uproar over his failure to attend the Fourth of July celebration at Independence Hall, was there to conclude what he had begun and to perhaps bathe in some of the glory of the Centennial before leaving office in a few months.

Closing day was less of an international affair than opening day. Emperor Dom Pedro was gone. The day belonged to those handful of people on the platform who had worked so long and so hard to bring the Centennial about and to make it a success. All were given their just due there on the platform with the President and the governors of several states.

Justice was further served for Women's Committee President Mrs. Gillespie. Just before the ceremony began, someone whispered to Hawley, master of ceremonies, and Mrs. Gillespie was moved from a back row on the platform to the front row with President Grant and the others most responsible for the success of the Centennial.

Because of the very limited space inside the

Judges' Pavilion, admission was granted only to dignitaries and those holding the special guest tickets to the closing ceremony. Most of the people waiting in the pouring rain were unaware of the late change of plans, and continued to wait long after the ceremony had begun.

Immediately after President Grant's arrival at 2 P.M., the orchestra struck up Wagner's Centennial March, which had been played for the first time on opening day. It may well have been the last time the mediocre tune was played, which is said to have made the composer very happy.

The first speaker was Pennsylvania Congressman and Centennial commissioner Daniel Morrell, who on March 9, 1870, had introduced the bill in Congress creating the Centennial. He chided the federal government for being so slow to fully support the project in deed and in dollars.

Midway through his remarks he spoke a prophesy for those of foresight to ponder: "The managers of future Centennial celebrations to be held on these grounds will see and do things more wonderful than our wildest dreams, and the remnants of our finest things may be exhibited by them as proofs of the rudeness of early days. . . ."

John Welsh, president of the Centennial Board of Finance, spoke next, followed by Director-General Goshorn and General Hawley. After Hawley's remarks, the audience joined in singing "America."

At this precise moment, a 47-gun salute, one for each state and territory, was fired from George's Hill and simultaneously from the U.S.S. Plymouth on the Delaware River. As the guns boomed in the distance, President Grant arose and said, "Ladies and gentlemen, I have now the honor to declare the Exhibition closed."

A nearby telegrapher tapped out the characters "7-6" to the main telegraph office. From there the following dispatch was placed on the wires to all the principal cities of the United States, Canada and Europe: "International Centennial Exhibition Grounds, Philadelphia, November 10, 1876. The President has this moment closed the International Exhibition: 3:37 P.M."

Over in Machinery Hall a crowd of approximately 15,000 had gathered around the Corliss Engine, fully expecting the President to come by to throw the switch to stop the engine, as he and Dom Pedro had done to start it at the opening of the Centennial.

However, as pre-arranged, the big engine was silenced by two engineers upon the sounding of a gong activated by the same "7-6" telegraph message that told the world the Centennial was over.

But the Centennial, like the big Corliss Engine, didn't cease immediately at 3:37 P.M. on November 10. It had great momentum, and had to wind down slowly.

On November 11, 15,000 people paid their way through the turnstiles for one more glimpse at all that had fascinated nearly 10 million visitors for the last six months. The following day the Centennial management opened the grounds to the public free for a rare Sunday visit. The buildings were closed, however.

People continued to pay admission to the fairgrounds for several weeks, with daily attendance averaging several thousand. As the weather grew colder the attendance dropped off to a few hundred a day, and finally in December the flow of people had stopped and the Centennial was closed.

Most visitors to the Centennial bemoaned the fact that all of the money and effort put into the Exhibition was only for a six-month show, and its wondrous buildings, except for two, were to be torn down.

With the fabulous up-swing in attendance through September, October and right up until the last day on November 10, serious consideration was being given to continuing the International Exhibition by reopening the next spring, sort of a "Centennial-plus-one" celebration.

The public was eager to see the Centennial continue. The Fairmount Park Commissioners, some of whom had foreseen this "problem" of permanent encroachment, had to be convinced. The plan, as set forth by a group of Philadelphia businessmen led by Clement M. Biddle and others who were involved in the Centennial, was to purchase the Main Exhibition Building and operate it as a Permanent International Exhibition.

Stock in the new enterprise was to be sold at $100 per share for a total capital investment of $600,000. By the end of the year almost the entire amount had been pledged.

Getting the Park Commission's approval and

The closing ceremonies were held in the Judges' Pavilion because of heavy rains.

raising the money were two major prerequisites for the new Permanent International Exhibition Company. Two others were the purchase of the building and the solicitation of permanent exhibitors.

On December 1, 1876, as required by law, a number of the principal Centennial buildings were sold at auction. The Main Exhibition Building was purchased by the Permanent International Exhibition Company for $250,000.

The task of soliciting permanent exhibitors was begun with the distribution of a circular to all exhibitors who had taken part in the Centennial. The invitations sought exhibitors in the areas of mining, manufacturing, education, science, art, machinery, agriculture and horticulture.

Most of the exhibitors had benefited so greatly from the Centennial that they were quick to accept the invitation for the permanent exhibition. By the end of the year all available space in the 21-acre building was spoken for. Many of those accepting were foreign merchants and manufacturers from the Centennial and new ones, thus assuring the international flavor of the permanent exhibition.

The exhibition was to re-open on May 1, 1877, but in order to coincide with the scheduled re-opening of the Art Gallery in Memorial Hall the new exhibition opened on May 10, the anniversary of the start of the Centennial.

President Rutherford B. Hayes, who had been inaugurated just two months earlier after winning the disputed and closest election on record from Samuel J. Tilden, was present at the opening ceremony. So was ex-President Grant.

Unfortunately, the Permanent International Exhibition Company quickly became involved in financial difficulties. In mid-summer Biddle retired from the management of the company, followed quickly by others in the organization. The exhibition floundered on under changing leadership, and by the end of the season was deep in debt. Many of the foreign exhibitors became disenchanted and pulled out.

However, the exhibition continued to operate for two more years through the summers of 1878 and 1879, at times attracting as many as 20,000 people on big days. Finally the Park Commission complained about the manner in which the permanent exhibition was being conducted. Apparently one of the most objectionable uses to which the building and park were being put was an annual farm show with a number of pig pens erected in the park.

The Park Commission ruled that the terms of the agreement with the original managers had been broken, and orders were given to vacate the building, a liberal two year notice being given.

Some public meetings were held to protest the closing, but in 1881 the project was finally at an end and the demolition of the mammoth building was begun.

The party was, at last, over.

8

CLEANING UP AFTER THE PARTY

The rules governing world's fairs call for the buildings or pavilions to be temporary structures to be removed at the close of the fair, and the area they occupied to be restored for park or other civic purposes. So it was with the Centennial.

On December 1, 1876, an auction was conducted to dispose of most of the Centennial buildings.

Aside from the buildings, most of the exhibition materials were either sold off during the final days of the Centennial or were returned to the nations, states and manufacturers which had exhibited them.

But 42 freight car loads of Centennial material, mostly from the United States and foreign pavilions, went to the Smithsonian Institution in Washington, D. C., as a gift. This large and significant gift prompted Congress to allocate funds to construct the National Museum, which later became the Arts and Industries Building of the Smithsonian.

The great Corliss Engine was purchased by the Pullman Company and operated much of the machinery in its Chicago shops for many years thereafter.

Of the 249 buildings on the Centennial grounds only Memorial Hall and Horticultural Hall were intended to remain after the Centennial as permanent buildings dedicated to public purposes.

A number of the smaller buildings were pur-

The Ohio House (above) and Memorial Hall (left) are the only buildings remaining from the Centennial. Both are open to visitors, with Ohio House serving as the Fairmount Park Information Center.

chased and moved to other locations. The State of Maryland removed its small building from the Centennial grounds and placed it in Druid Hill Park in Baltimore, where it still stands. Demolition of the enormous Main Exhibition Hall was finally begun in 1881.

The U. S. Life-Saving Services Building, located next to Centennial Lake, was bought by a church group to become St. Peter's By-the-Sea Church in Cape May Point, New Jersey. The tiny building, or a replica, still stands in that South Jersey community.

The Centennial Catalogue Building was picked up and transported to the Philadelphia Main Line community of Strafford, where it was converted into a Pennsylvania Railroad station. It is still in use today.

The Wisconsin Building was purchased by an ill-fated concern that managed to move it only half a mile from the fairgrounds before running out of money. There it sat abandoned for more than a year before someone else finally purchased it and moved it to the nearby suburb of

Bala, where it served as a small hotel called the Wisconsin House. It was razed in 1961. The Michigan Building was purchased by a Philadelphia man and transported to Atlantic City, New Jersey, to serve as a summer residence. It was later a guest house called States Villa, and was destroyed by fire in 1954.

The English Building remained on its original site in Fairmount Park and served for many years as a park maintenance office and a residence for park employees. It was torn down in 1961.

Horticultural Hall served as a popular botanical exhibition hall for the City of Philadelphia under the management of the Park Commission for almost 80 years after the Centennial. The building, which was made entirely of glass and iron, fell into disrepair during the Depression and the Second World War. In 1954 it was damaged by Hurricane Hazel, and the decision was made to tear it down. Demolition occurred in 1955.

Memorial Hall remains, as intended, a memorium to the 100th anniversary of the founding of the United States and to the celebration held to commemorate that event in 1876. Throughout most of its life the building served as an art museum and art school, being the home of the Pennsylvania Museum and School of Industrial Arts for many years.

In the 1920s, when the Benjamin Franklin Parkway was developed and the Philadelphia Museum of Art was completed at the head of the Parkway, most of the major art works were transferred from Memorial Hall to the new museum. In 1954 an auction was held in Memorial Hall to dispose of the remaining exhibit materials. Over the decade from 1958 until 1968 the City of Philadelphia spent $1,500,000 (ironically, the same amount it cost to construct the building in 1875-1876) to restore the structure as a combined headquarters for the Fairmount Park Commission and the Fairmount Park Guard, a public recreation center with an indoor swimming pool and basketball court, and a social hall for city functions to be held in "The Great Hall" rotunda area under the beautiful double glass dome.

Of all the temporary buildings of the Centennial, only the Ohio House remains intact on its original location on Belmont Avenue at States Drive. A very substantial struc-

The Wisconsin Building (left) was moved to Bala, Pa., where it became a hotel. The English Building (right) remained in the park until 1961, when it was demolished.

ture of native Ohio stone, the building served for most of its post-Centennial life as a park employee's residence and was refurbished to serve as a park information center in 1976.

Several of the statues and fountains of the Centennial also still remain in the park.

*   *   *

The fact that the United States had survived for a century was, in the minds of many, ample reason for a celebration in 1876. It had not been an easy hundred years, but then no one had thought it would be.

Aside from the growing pains of expanding from a loosely knit federation of 13 colonies along the Atlantic seaboard to a vast transcontinental nation, the War Between the States had almost dealt the union a killing blow. One hundred miles west of the Centennial grounds lay 4500 dead soldiers, all Americans, over whom Abraham Lincoln had eulogized four score and seven years after the events being celebrated in Philadelphia in 1876.

Much more than a celebration of endurance took place in Philadelphia in 1876, however. In fact, few remind-

ers of the struggles of the previous century could be found at the Centennial.

The painting of "The Spirit of '76," George Washington's carriage and battle gear, and Ben Franklin's original printing press were among the few reminders of the men and events of a hundred years before.

Of the great Civil War, only the tall, mute white marble figure of "The American Volunteer" and the ornery Wisconsin war eagle "Old Abe" reminded Centennial visitors of the recent and painful confrontation.

The Centennial was a celebration of the future more than a reflection of the past. Like all world's fairs, it was to tell the world of the great things to come: the great machines to do the work of many men, the telephone to join distant peoples for the first time and the monorail which was hailed as the transportation of the future.

But above all, the Centennial introduced the United States to the nations of the world as a new and equal partner. The Colonies had grown up, and the 100 candles on the Centennial birthday cake in Philadelphia in 1876 cast a giant glow across the face of the globe that had not been there before.

✿ THE AUTHOR

Richard R. Nicolai was born in Philadelphia in 1932, and he has remained a Philadelphian by choice ever since. He is Information Officer for the Fairmount Park Commission, which operates the largest municipal park in the world, and his office is in Memorial Hall, the last major building remaining from the Centennial.

Mr. Nicolai is a graduate of Temple University. He served in the Army during the Korean War. Prior to joining the Park Commission, he was a sports writer for The Philadelphia Inquirer.

He lives in the Bridesburg section of Philadelphia with his wife Florence, his daughter, his mother-in-law and a beagle named Max.

✿ THE ILLUSTRATIONS

All drawings are from *Frank Leslie's Illustrated Historical Register of the Centennial Exposition* and all photographs are from the Free Library of Philadelphia, with the following exceptions: Page 1, Collection of Oresto Bucciero; Page 16, Harper's Weekly; Page 33, Peterson's Magazine; Page 36, City of Philadelphia Records Department, Archives Division; Page 37, Harper's Weekly; Page 50 (right), Harper's Weekly; Page 52 (top left), Historical Society of Pennsylvania; Page 54, Collection of Richard R. Nicolai; Page 82, Harper's Weekly; Page 83, Collection of Ronald DeGraw; Page 84, Harper's Weekly; and Page 92, Philadelphia Electric Company. The drawing on the cover is from the Harper's Weekly issue of May 27, 1876.

✿ THE BOOK

The text of this book is set in 11-point Melior Roman, leaded one point, and the captions are in 9-point Melior Italic. The chapter headings are 30-point Davida Bold. The paper is 80-pound Karma Text. Typesetting and printing are by Waldman Graphics, Inc., of Philadelphia, and binding is by Complete Books Company, of Philadelphia. The book was designed by Ronald DeGraw.